Bake For Profit
- Start a home business -

Nick van der Walt

Copyright © 2017 T N van der Walt

All rights reserved.

ISBN:9781719947039
ISBN-13:

LEGAL NOTICE

While the author has attempted to be as accurate and complete as possible, he assumes no responsibility for errors, omissions or contrary interpretation of the subject matter.

This book is not intended for use as a source of legal, business or financial advice.

Any earnings or income statements are only estimates of what the author thinks you can earn. There is no assurance that you will achieve this income. The financial figures in this book are illustrative only and do not necessarily reflect the real prices and value of products.

You are NOT licensed to resell, loan, give away or auction this book without the specific written consent of the author.

All rights reserved.

CONTENTS

Page

1	Start a Home Baking Business	1
2	Home Baking Basics	7
3	How to Calculate Production Cost	19
4	Profitable Starter Recipes	30
5	How to Promote Your Product	42
6	How to Find a Market	46
7	Home Baking Resources	49
8	Conclusions	54
9	About the Author	55

1. START A HOME BAKING BUSINESS

Have you considered utilizing your baking skills to develop the easiest and most lucrative home business? Then you should be thinking of starting a cookie and candy business from your own home. Everybody loves cookies and candy and if it is homemade, it adds that extra attraction. A stake in the cookie and candy market can be very lucrative, as well as rewarding for you and your wallet. So if you are looking for a great business opportunity, why not try your hand at selling cookies and candy?

The current trend is towards more home-based businesses. They require lower overhead and startup money making them easier for entrepreneurs with limited funds. There are several benefits to running a home-based baking business. First of all, you can run the business from your home. Since you already pay a mortgage, utilities and car payments, the only thing you need spend money on now is the equipment for your business.

Secondly, a home-based business requires low overhead and startup costs. The key to keeping the overhead low is taking on only as much as you can safely and efficiently handle by yourself. Try to do as many things yourself rather than appointing extra staff.

Another important factor is the fact that you can start small and develop your skills and establish a market for your products. A home business allows you to turn a hobby or a passion into money making endeavor. It can provide a handsome additional income or even develop into a full time business. Home baking for a profit is a popular business the world over and has been practiced for many generations. If you love baking, a home bake business is ideal to start because you already have a kitchen and most of the tools and equipment needed to start your business.

There are literally thousands and thousands of styles and combinations for business ideas that can make you very successful. What about a cupcake business? You can make money by making cupcakes at home and selling them at community events. What about a cake decorating business? You could also go with a basic sugar cookie recipe, but cut them out into all different shapes, sizes and decorations to go with every holiday or occasion. You may want to target a unique niche market such as sugar free cookies and candy for diabetics. If you are a dog or cat lover, you may want to start making gourmet dog and cat food. The opportunities are endless.

In the cookie business, it is easy to see that such cheap ingredients such as flour, sugar, eggs, and other flavorings can easily be turned into a product that is not only eye catching and tasty, but also one that can bring in a fabulous stream of income for years and years to come.

Items to consider before starting

1. What type of product is permitted for home baking?

Before you get started with a home based baking business, you should be aware of the fact that in some areas, local authority- and health laws set certain standards that have to be met before you can start a home bake business. In some instances you are only allowed to produce so-called ***non-potentially hazardous food*** without a permit. ***Potentially hazardous*** food must be certified by the authorities and a permit issued before you can produce and sell these products. Products such as meat and meat products, fish, dairy products and products requiring refrigeration fall under this category.

Potentially non-hazardous food is defined as foods that do not easily support the growth of dangerous bacteria and do not require refrigeration to control safety. It makes sense to stick to exempted products such as the following:

Baked goods such as cookies, breads and cakes but excludes baked goods containing cream-based fillings, whipped cream, and toppings requiring refrigeration.

Bottled/Jarred items such as jams, pickles, relishes, juices etc.

Candies/Confections such as hard candies, fudge, truffles, brittles, chocolate covered candy and fruit, marshmallows etc.

Fermented products such as fermented fruit and vegetable products

Other products such as dehydrated fruit and vegetables, dried herbs, nuts, roasted coffee and dried tea etc.

2. Exemption requirements

Some authorities may also have certain conditions that must be complied with – even if you make and sell exempted products. Some of these conditions may include the following:

- The recipe must be available at all times should there be a concern about safety of the product
- Restrictions regarding the processing, packaging and selling of the product
- Gross sales per year may be restricted
- The kitchen must be inspected and certified as approved
- Labeling must contain certain information such as the name and address of the producer. Where products contain allergens such as wheat, eggs, dairy etc. it must be specified on the label.

In the light of these requirements it would be wise to carefully consider the type of product that you produce from your home.

Start-up checklist

The following checklist may be helpful in setting up your home business.

Step 1 – Decide what product you are going to produce

Cookies and candy are always popular and fall in the low risk category and should be seriously considered.

Step 2 – Verify that your product can be produced at home

Contact your local food and health department to find out what conditions apply to home-based cookie production.

Step 3 – Verify that your kitchen can be used to manufacture your product.

Kitchen requirements can include aspects such as:

- No pets allowed in the home

- Easily cleanable working surfaces

- Restroom and hand washing facilities must be readily available

- Hot and cold water must be available with a proper drainage system

Step 4 – Check the local authority for licensing and zoning requirements

Legalize your business and start on the right footing.

Step 5 – Learn how to make your product safely

Make sure that you understand the recipe and that the end product meets your standard.

Step 6 - Develop your business plan

The following details should be included:

- Description of the product(s) that you will be manufacturing

- Detailed recipe(s) setting out the ingredients, and the procedure

- A plan for storing supplies, equipment and the finished product

- How the product will be transported

- Potential locations to sell the product

- Set out the selling price and the estimated sales in the next 6 – 12 months

- A marketing plan

In chapter 7 you will find more details on drawing up a business plan.

Step 7 – Choose appropriate packaging and design a label

The label should include the following information:

- Product name
- Manufacturer name and address
- Net weight of the product in ounces or gram weight equivalent
- List of ingredients

Other considerations

There are some other considerations before beginning any type of business even a home-based one such as baking cookies and making candy:

- Are you a complete novice in baking or do you have some experience? To be successful you must have an interest in baking and a desire to be a successful baker. There are other home businesses that you may want to explore before a final decision is made. Talk to people who are involved in a similar business and get unbiased opinions before you proceed. Visit farmer's markets and check out what other people are doing.
- Do you have a suitable kitchen or other work area? Do you have refrigeration and storage facilities? Do you have small kids and will you be able to devote enough time to the business?
- What do family and friends think of your product? If they like it you may have a winner.

OK. So you have decided that home baking is what you want to do! The first step is to make a final decision on the type of product/s that you will be manufacturing.

Why cookies and candy?

As was mentioned, there are many options when you are considering a home bake business. To make money from your efforts, there are some principles that you should consider.

Firstly, you want to make money! Cookies and candy allow you to utilize the following key ingredients which are necessary in any successful business:

Cost-effectiveness. The cost of ingredients and other inputs should allow you to charge a reasonable selling price and in turn provide a profit. Later in Chapter 3 you will be provided with a price calculating tool to assist you in properly pricing your product. Cookies and candy can be produced cost-effectively (provided you have the right recipes) and you can make a handsome profit.

Attractive product. With some extra effort you can decorate your product to make it attractive. Quality packaging is most important. An attractive product will create a desire to buy and make it easy to sell.

Quality product. With quality ingredients you can create products that will make your customers want to come back for more. A tasty cookie or candy will give you a happy customer.

Secondly, you want a product that has a reasonable shelf life. Products such as cakes and pies must be sold immediately. Cookies and candy on the other hand, can be stored or even refrigerated to last for a long time. What you don't sell today, you can sell tomorrow or next week. You will find some tips on storing your cookies in chapter 7.

Thirdly, most cookies and candy can withstand reasonably rough handling. If you are going to transport or ship your product, you want to be sure that it reaches its destination intact.

Fourthly, everybody likes cookies and candy, and they are really versatile and you can let your imagination go. Cookie hampers or gift baskets are popular and you can establish a lucrative corporate market. Fortune cookies and wedding gift cookies are ideal for special occasions such as birthdays and weddings. You can also meet the special needs of some of your customers. Special diabetic cookies or diet cookies can provide you with a niche that can be a money spinner.

Lastly, to make cookies and candy, you don't need specialized equipment or knowledge. It is the ideal home business. Use your baking skills (even if it is limited) and make real money. Your potential market starts with your close friends and family. Making money was never easier and I will show you how to start and build your business.

2. HOME BAKING BASICS

1. General

Before starting your business, it is important that you try out the recipes that I provide in Chapter 4. Take them for a test drive and make sure that you understand all the directions. This is particularly true when you are making candy from sugar syrup and you want to make sure that your mixture reaches the required temperature before removing it from the heat.

You also want to make sure that your cookies are of high quality before you go out and present them to prospective customers. It is a good idea to let somebody you trust, give you an honest opinion about your products.

Make sure that you measure the ingredients accurately. It helps to have the ingredients in the order that you are going to use them. First put out ALL the ingredients and then measure them before mixing. Do not over mix the dough. Do not over bake. Keep to the recipe. Select the correct measurement utensils. Make sure that eggs and butter are at room temperature before mixing.

To cut hard candy such as peanut brittle, it should be done before the mixture has cooled down completely. Mark out the pieces to the exact size (5cm x 8cm) and cut through with a sharp knife. When the mixture has cooled down to room temperature, break in pieces.

To cut soft candy such as Turkish delight and marshmallows, regularly soak the knife in hot water and lightly wipe the blade. A few drops of cooking oil on the blade will also prevent the knife from sticking to the mixture. Measure the pieces to be cut with a ruler and cut through with a sharp knife.

Basic Guidelines for Baking Cookies

Cookies are easy to make but to sell them some extra effort should be put in. Well decorated and attractive cookies nicely presented will always find a buyer. Here are some basic tips to make life easier when you start out with your cookie baking:

- Make sure the cookie dough is at room temperature before baking. Chilling the dough means that the dough takes longer to melt, letting the heat of the oven set the crust before the cookie has fully spread.

- Instead of greasing your baking pans, use baking paper. You will find it in any grocery store and it will save you a lot of time. You just tear off a sheet, place it in the pan and you can start baking. You can also use the sheet for a number of times before having to replace it with a new one. Cookies do not stick to it, and it makes it easier to take them off the pan to put them on cooling racks.

- Use a heavy roll pin to roll out dough. Get a piece of transparent plastic table cloth of about 1m x 0.5 m to work on. Lightly sprinkle some flour to avoid the dough from sticking to the plastic sheet.

- Use a teaspoon or even a melon scoop to scoop the dough in even lumps for placement on the baking sheet. Try to make sure that all your cookies are the same size and thickness. Do not make it too thick because you want your cookies to be crispy (about 3 mm).

- Place the balls of dough 2 to 3 cm apart to allow for cookies to spread out. Press each ball lightly with your thumb to make a small dent. You can also use a fork but this might leave fork marks on the baked cookies.

- When making cookie dough that has to be chilled, chill it in log shapes. Take a piece of wax wrap paper and put a roll of dough in the paper. Now start shaping it into a log shape and fold it close with the paper for easy refrigeration. When the dough is in log shapes, all you have to do is slice and bake. The cookies will come out in uniform slices for cooking evenly and makes it easy to place on a cookie sheet and bake them faster. They also hold their shape better.

- Always preheat your oven. This will ensure that the cookies start baking immediately and evenly.

- Set your oven's heat to the desired level and also time your baking. Frequently check to make sure that cookies are baking evenly.

- Make sure your oven is registering the correct temperature. Sometimes ovens get out of sync with what temperature you set it to and what it actually heats up to. If there is doubt if your oven is registering the correct temperature, then put a thermometer inside the oven and heat it up. Then, read the temperature on the thermometer and make sure it is right. If it is wrong, either calibrate your oven by the oven manual's directions, have it serviced by a trained technician, or adjust the temperature to where it is registering the right temperature that you need so you can bake your cookies. Then have it looked at later. Nothing is worse than not knowing that your oven is at the wrong temperature until your cookies come out burnt to a crisp or barely cooked at all.

- Make sure the oven rack is in the center position before turning on your oven. Oven rack placement is vital to cookies either being burnt on the bottom from it being too low and not cooked on the top or not getting all the way done because the rack is too high. Such an easy tip that many overlook until they are wondering what is wrong with their cookies.
- Let the cookies stand about 1-2 minutes before removing them to wire cooling racks. This allows the cookies to settle and harden a little bit so they are easier to remove from the cookie sheet. If you remove them too soon, they fall apart.
- You can freeze cookie dough. If you want homemade cookies, but do not want so many of them all at once; then you can freeze the dough. Get yourself a food sealer and some bags or canisters that you can vacuum seal and you are in business. Stores are also selling a do it yourself sealer that does a wonderful job of vacuum sealing bags for a lower cost than buying a regular sealer, That way your cookie dough doesn't get freezer burned and you can just bake a few at a time, rather than have 5 dozen cookies laying around.
- This one is probably the no-brainer of the bunch...FOLLOW THE RECIPE EXACTLY. Many times cookies do not turn out because a person did not follow their recipe. The person who made the recipe knows how much of dry ingredients versus wet ingredients go together to make a cookie dough that comes out of the oven into edible cookies. Trust them. Do not start substituting ingredients to make it low fat or reduced sugar or something else, because chances are it will not turn out. Do not substitute applesauce for butter or cake flour for all purpose flour, because they are different densities and it will make your cookie flop.

- **Tip:**
  Sifting Dry Ingredients: It is always better to sift any dry ingredients, especially flour and powdered sugar, before adding them. Sifting can be done by using a fine mesh sieve.

Baking Tools and Equipment for Cookies

Baking homemade cookies is a lot more enjoyable when you have the right tools and equipment. Here's a list of items that will help insure cookie baking success.

- **Baking Pans and Cookie Sheets**: Come in a wide variety of styles and materials. Dark metal pans absorb heat and will cause cookies and brownies to brown more quickly. Shiny metal pans reflect heat making them perfect for more delicate baked treats. Air-cushioned sheets provide extra protection from burning but make it difficult to obtain golden brown cookies. Glass pans carry heat more effectively so your oven temperature needs to be adjusted down 25 degrees when using them. Basic pan sizes you'll want in your collection include:

    9 x 13-inch

    8-inch square

    9-inch square

    9-inch round

- **Bowls**: Small, medium, and large mixing bowls in glass or stainless steel.
- **Wooden Spoons**: Great for stirring batter
- **Measuring Spoons**: One or two sets of graduated spoons designed specifically for measuring
- **Measuring Cups**: A 2-cup glass or plastic one for liquids that has a spout and a set of dry graduated measuring cups
- **Spatulas**: One thin metal spatula for removing cookies from the pan and a couple of plastic spatulas for working with chocolate.

- **Whisks**: One or two medium to large whisks for mixing both dry and wet ingredients
- **Parchment Paper** (Baking paper): An indispensable aid for quick and easy baking. It is available in both rolls and sheets.
- **Wire Racks**: For cooling your cookies.
- **Electric Mixer**: You should have both a hand held mixer and a stand-alone table model
- **Digital kitchen scale** – invest in a scale that can weigh small amounts of yeast and salt and precise enough to weigh tenths of grams. Accuracy in adding the correct amount of ingredients can make a big difference in the taste of a cookie or candy.

Basic Guidelines to Make Candy

Making candy requires a special touch. The following are some basic guidelines to help you be a successful candy maker.

How to Use a Candy Thermometer

If you use a thermometer it must measure up to 180°C (350°F) or higher. Test the thermometer before use by placing it in water and then bring the water to boil. The temperature of the water should be 100°C or 212°F at the coast. Make the necessary adjustments for places above sea level which should be a lower boiling point. The boiling point of water drops about 1°C (2°F) for every 300 m above sea level.

To prevent the glass of the thermometer to crack, first submerge into a glass of boiling water before putting it into boiling sugar syrup. After removing from the boiling syrup, place the thermometer back into the glass with hot water to cool down.

To get the best results, a candy thermometer is essential. However, if you don't have one, don't worry, the recipes that you will use are very simple and you can get away without using a thermometer by doing the cold water test.

How to Use the Cold Water Test

The cold water test can be performed to test the temperature of the mixture. Take a teaspoon full of boiling syrup and drop it into a bowl of very cold water. Put your hand in the water and make the drop into a ball. The degree of stiffness of the ball will give an indication of the temperature of the mixture.

Note of Caution: Please be careful when working with boiling sugar. It is extremely hot and care should be taken to avoid spilling and burning yourself.

The *candy temperature chart* gives the different stages of sugar syrup and there uses in making different types of candy.

1. ***Thread stage*** (230°F -234°F) (110°C-112°C) - This is where the syrup drips from the spoon.
2. ***Soft ball stage*** (234°F-239°F) (112°C - 115°C) - Syrup forms a ball in the water but flattens when removed. Used for glazed and candied fruits, fudge, fondant.
3. ***Firm ball stage*** (244°F-248°F) (118°C - 120°C) - Syrup forms firm ball but loses shape. Used for soft caramels and marshmallows.
4. ***Hard ball stage*** (250°F-266°F) (121°C - 130°C) - Syrup holds ball shape but remains sticky. Used for nougat and divinity.
5. ***Soft crack stage*** (270°F-289°F) (132°C - 143°C) - Syrup will form firm but pliable threads. Used for taffy.
6. ***Hard crack stage*** (300°F-309°F) (149°C - 154°C) - Syrup will crack if you try to form it. Used for brittles, toffees and lollipops.
7. ***Caramel*** (320°F-370°F) (160°C-189°C). For praline.

Note: Temperatures are accurate at sea level.

Here are some tips for making sugar syrup.

- Pre-warm your thermometer before inserting it in the hot syrup.

- Regularly wash down the sugar crystals from the side of the pan. This prevents crystallization of the sugar.

- Always use a wooden spoon to stir the syrup. Metal spoons heat quickly and may burn the syrup. Cold metal may cause premature precipitation, cooling down the syrup.

The taste of candy must be delicate and when adding flavoring, use a medicine dripper. Mix all the ingredients thoroughly before boiling. Gently stir the sugar over low heat until dissolved. Do not stir when boiling starts. While the syrup is boiling, the sugar crystals must be removed from the sides of the pan. Use a small brush dipped into water to brush the sides of the sauce pan. Candy that contain cream, butter, syrup or chocolates, will rise when boiling, so make sure that the sauce pan is big enough.

The addition of glucose syrup will ensure a fine texture candy. Crème of tartar and vinegar will give the same result but be careful not to add too much as this will prevent the candy from becoming stiff enough.

When the syrup has reached the desired temperature, remove the sauce pan from the heat and put into cold water so that the temperature does not rise any further.

Types of Candy

Candy is basically made from two sources. The first is a **sugar** water mixture or syrup and the second is **chocolate.**

I like to divide *sugar candies* into the following basic types:

- Hard candies such as brittles and lollipops. Peanut brittle is a favorite that we recommend for your cookie/candy business. The sugar mixture is hard and cracks when cold. They can be colored and flavored in wide variety. Moulds can be used to make them in different forms.

- Toffee and caramel are made in the same way as hard candy except that milk and fat are added. The milk is usually condensed milk and the fat is either butter or vegetable oil.

- Nougat is placed in a separate category because it doesn't contain milk and it is aerated by mixing egg in boiled syrup. It is a tricky process and not recommended for beginners.
- Soft candies such as marshmallows and Turkish delight. This is where the syrup holds its ball shape but is still sticky. They are not difficult to make and are recommended for home baking.
- Jelly candies. These are made of gelatin and they have a chewy texture and are often flavored with fruit juices or extracts.

Working with Chocolate

Working with chocolate requires a skill to melt the chocolate. You will need some experience to do this, but once acquired, there are many possibilities for working with chocolate.

There are some tricks to successfully melting chocolate. Whether you are working with dark, semisweet, milk, or white chocolate, here are some tips to follow.

- Never allow any *water* to come in contact with the melting chocolate, unless the chocolate is being melted in a large amount of water (2 tablespoons water per ounce of chocolate is the minimum amount). Just a drop or two of water can make the chocolate seize up, or become hard and lumpy. Even the steam from the bottom of a double boiler can cause this problem. Make sure to keep the chocolate dry as it melts. If it does seize, you can blend in a teaspoon of vegetable oil (NOT butter or margarine) and the chocolate should smooth out.
- Chocolate should only be melted over *low heat*. The microwave is a good appliance to use because the cooking time is so controlled. If you stand at the stove and stir constantly, you can melt chocolate in a pan set over very low heat. A double boiler (watch out for condensation) is a good method; make sure the water in the bottom is barely simmering.
- White chocolate or vanilla milk chips are the most difficult to melt. Too much heat will make this type of chocolate seize.
- To melt chocolate bars in a microwave, first coarsely chop the chocolate. Place in a microwave safe bowl and heat on 50% power

for 1 minute. Remove from the microwave and stir. Continue this process until the chocolate is almost melted. Then stir until the chocolate is smooth.

- Melt chocolate chips just like chopped bars. To make a dipping chocolate for coating candies, when the chocolate is almost melted add ¼ cup more chips and stir constantly until the mixture is smooth. This will help set up sugar crystals so the chocolate stays firm at room temperature.

Baking Tools for Making Candy

In general, candy making does not require much in the way of specialized equipment. Many candies can be made using basic kitchen tools that most people already possess. But there are a few tools that reappear in recipes over and over again, like a candy thermometer, and it will be helpful to familiarize yourself with the most commonly used candy and chocolate equipment.

Candy Thermometer

The candy thermometer is probably the single most important piece of equipment for the home confectioner. Many recipes require candy to be cooked to a specific temperature in order for the candy to behave and set properly. Although it is possible to make candy without a thermometer using the so-called cold water testing method, a thermometer makes things infinitely easier, and can be purchased cheaply at most major grocery stores. If you will be making candy frequently, it is a good idea to invest in a high-quality thermometer.

The most important thing to look for in a thermometer is a side clip that allows it to attach to your saucepans so that your hands remain free while making candy. You want to attach your thermometer to the side of the pan with the tip fully immersed in the candy, but not touching the bottom of the pan.

Dipping Instruments

Dipping instruments for candy can range from simple dinner forks, to inexpensive plastic instruments, to pricey metal hand-crafted tools.

Although you can dip truffles and other candy using your fingers or dinner forks, the specialized shape of dipping tools makes it easier to produce a smooth, professional candy. Instruments vary in size and shape depending on the candy or fruit to be dipped. A variety of tools can generally be found at craft or cake/candy supply stores.

Pastry bags

Pastry bags and tips are useful for filling molds or delicate candies with small openings. Often, candies can be filled using a spoon, but this tends to create a bit of a mess, especially if the candy opening is small or the filling is sticky. Pastry bags eliminate much of the mess and speed up the filling process. Bags and tips are also good for adding decorative touches to candies using icing, chocolate, or other confections.

To produce the *Money Maker Candy Recipes* recommended in this book, you will require the following pans and equipment:

- Small saucepans 18cm x 27 cm x 2.5 cm deep.
- Heavy saucepan to boil sugar mixtures
- Electric hand mixer
- Candy thermometer
- Cup measures
- Tablespoon and teaspoon measures
- Kitchen scale

Types of cookies

A handy classification of the types of cookies can be made by how they are formed.

1. Drop cookies
Drop cookies are made with a creamed batter that can be dropped with a teaspoon on a prepared cookie sheet. This is an easy type of cookie to make – just mix, drop and bake. Drop cookie dough can vary in texture from quite stiff to soft. Some popular types of drop cookies include peanut butter cookies, oatmeal raisin cookies, and old fashioned sugar cookies.

The dough can also be chilled in the freezer and then formed into balls that are slightly flattened before baking.

2. Rolled and shaped cookies

This category includes cookies that are cut out and sliced. The dough is chilled before slicing or cutting. They can be shaped by hand or by using cutters or moulds. Ginger cookies and traditional Christmas cookies are examples.

3. Refrigerator or icebox cookies

These cookies are made of stiff dough and must be refrigerated before use. The dough is shaped into logs and chilled before slicing. The dough can be kept in the refrigerator and then sliced and bake.

4. Bar cookies or squares

It is an easy cookie to bake. The dough is poured or pressed into a pan and after the bake process and it is cooled it is cut into cookie-sized pieces. Brownies are a classic example.

5. Piped cookies

Pied cookies require the most care and precision. The dough temperature is crucial. It is essential that the butter be cool and not too soft (60°F to 65°F).

6. Biscotti

This biscuit has its origin in Italy. It is a hard, crisp cookie and is a twice-baked cookie. After baking, the biscotti are "dried" in a cool oven to get a crispy, crunchy end product. The addition of butter changes the texture from brittle and crisp to dry and crumbly. Nuts are usually added to dominate the flavor but dried fruit and raisins are popular alternatives. They can be stored for a long time and will retain its flavor if stored in an airtight container.

7. **Shortbread**

This traditional and very popular cookie is a simple formula of butter, sugar, flour and salt. Butter is the dominant flavor but many flavor variations can be achieved by adding chocolate, lemon, maple or oats. Most recipes are made up of a basic ratio of 2 cups of butter to 1 cup of sugar and 4 cups of flour. Additional ingredients are a matter of personal preference. The dough can be pressed into a pan or it can be chilled in a bar or log and cut into shape before baking.

3. HOW TO CALCULATE PRODUCTION COST AND SELLING PRICE

To calculate production cost and selling price of a product a standardized recipe makes it easy. It also helps to compare different recipes and to make informed decisions in choosing a profitable recipe.

Standardizing a recipe

It is important to standardize your recipes so that you get a uniform result every time. Be careful when making changes to a recipe. When you simply increase the quantities you may cause unforeseen reactions that may affect the end product. Be sure to first test the result before adopting a new recipe.

A standardized format is recommended to also comply with regulating authorities' requirements. Your recipe should include the following:

- Name of the product

- Yield – number of servings or volume or weight. I prefer the weight since it is the basis of calculating the selling price.

- Time to prepare and bake

- Ingredients in the order that it will be used

- Quantity of each ingredient in weight and volume

- Short and precise description of the procedure to be followed. Include a description of the preparation and combining of ingredients, baking method and temperature Tools and equipment required

- Size and number of pans required (state whether metal or glass)

- Tools and equipment]

- Packaging

The following is an example of a standardized recipe for shortbread cookies.

Name: Shortbread

This long time favorite is loved by everybody. Butter is the only flavoring in this cookie. You get sweetness from the sugar and the flour gives it body but it's the butter that supplies the taste. All true shortbread cookie recipes should include butter. Not lard, not butter flavored shortening and definitely not margarine but honest to goodness butter. It should also be the freshest butter you can find.

The cookies are made by chilling the dough in a log form and then cutting it into squares before baking.

Yield: 1200g of cookies

Prep time: 10 min

Bake time: 10 min

Total time: 20 min or 0.33hr

Ingredients:

500 g Butter

200g Castor sugar

500 g Flour (2 cups)

37.5 ml Corn flour

Procedure:

1. Mix castor sugar and butter.
2. Add flour and corn flour and mix in. Roll out dough in wax paper in sausage form.
3. Refrigerate until cold and dough is firm and holds shape. (1hr)
4. Cut in 0.5 cm slices and put on greased pan or baking sheets.

5. Bake at 180° C until light brown, for about 10 min.

6. Remove the pan from the oven and let it cool down on a cooling rack.

7. When cooled down, gently pack them in plastic buckets and seal with the lid.

8. Store in a cool place.

Tools and equipment:

1. Hand mixer or electric mixer
2. Metal pan 9 x 13 inches
3. Mixing bowl
4. Measuring cups
5. Wax paper
6. Baking paper
7. Wire racks for cooling

Packaging:

Four x 1 liter clear plastic buckets with lids.

Transportation:

Since shortbread is very brittle and can easily break during transportation it should be packed securely and handled with care.

Notes on standardization

To standardize a recipe it is also important to note the following:

- Ingredients are listed in the order in which you are going to use them
- Quantities are expressed in the smallest measurable unit such as

grams, ounces, milliliters etc. and units such as cups or tablespoons etc are avoided.

- Yield is expressed in weight or volume and not as a number of cookies.

As an example – when you buy a 3lb pack of cake flour at $17.50 per pack the unit of measurement is calculated as follows:

3 pounds = 48 ounces

48 ounces at $17.50 = $0.36 per ounce.

The measurement unit is indicated in ounces and the cost is $0.36/ounce.

By using a uniform measure, calculating ingredient cost becomes a breeze.

Cost Factors to Consider

The objective of your home baked cookie business is to make a reasonable profit. How do you determine the selling price? There are a number of factors to consider in determining the selling price.

Firstly, you have to know the *cost of your ingredients*. In this regard it is important to try and find the best price for a product and it will be worth your while to shop around to find the best prices. It is also important to use only recipes that will give you a good quality end product without using expensive ingredients. For instance, you can in many cases substitute butter with margarine at a substantially lower cost, without compromising the quality of the product.

Secondly, you need to know what *output quantity* you can achieve with a particular input or recipe. The quantity produced must be established by weighing the number of cookies produced with a specific set of ingredients. Now you can calculate the cost to produce the particular batch of cookies.

Thirdly, you should consider the *cost of packaging and labeling.* This is an important consideration because high quality packaging can give a professional and attractive look that will make your product sell. Be aware though, packaging and labeling can be expensive and can take a considerable chunk out of your potential profit.

Fourthly, you must determine your *labor cost*. Your labor cost will probably be considerably lower than what the bakery industry is paying. However, setting a realistic cost is essential because you might eventually consider employing somebody to assist you and building it in at an early stage will give you the opportunity to grow your business.

Lastly, you should consider your *overhead costs* such as electricity, transport and administrative cost...

How to calculate the selling price

It is very important to get the correct selling price for your product. The success of your business depends heavily on the amount of product you can sell. If your price is too high you will obviously not sell enough and if it is too low, you will not make a reasonable profit.

To calculate the selling price of your product you could use one of two methods that are generally used by the food industry. The first is the *production cost* method and the second is the *percentage* method.

a. Production Cost Method

To calculate production cost (the total cost to produce a product) you must know the number of units that you can produce in a certain period of time - using **productive working hours** or the total time you spend to make a certain product. For example, if you plan to work 8 hours a day for 3 days per week or 96 hours per month and you can produce 1750 gr cookies in an hour, the production cost can be calculated as follows:

Step 1 – Work out hours spent in actually making the product.

A distinction can be made between *production working hours* and *operational working hours*. Production time is the time spent to actually produce a product and operational time includes tasks such as marketing, bookkeeping, administration, shopping, delivery etc. If you spend 2 hours out of an 8 hr day (25%) on operational activities, your production hours are 6 hours(8 – 2 = 6) per day (75%) or **120 hrs** (6hrs x 20days = 120) per 20 day month. Your operational hours will be **40 hrs** (2 hrs x 20 days = 40) per month. If you decide on a total labor rate (production time plus operational time) of $5 per hour, then your production labor cost will be **$600** (120hrs x $5 = 600) and operational labor cost will be **$200** (40 x $5 = 200) per month. The total labor cost per month will be $800 per month ($600 + $200 = $800).

Since you are starting a home business you will most likely not be working 8 hrs per day for 20 or 21 days per month. Let us assume you will be working a total of 3 days per week (24 hrs) or 96 hrs per month (24 x 4 = 96). Your production labor hours will then be 72 hrs (75% of 96 hrs = 72) and your operational labor hrs will be 24 hrs (25% of 96 hrs = 24 hrs).

Production labor cost will be $360 (72 x $5 = 360)

Operational labor cost will be $120 (24 x $5 = 120)

To summarize:

Total production labor hours = 72 hours per month

Total operational labor hours = 24 hours per month

Total labor hours = 96 hours per month

Total labor production cost = $ 360 per month

Total labor operational cost = $ 120 per month

Total labor cost = $ 480 per month or $ 5 per hour

Step 2 – Determine other monthly costs such as electricity, transport etc.

Other monthly costs include items such as electricity, fuel, packaging, advertising, admin and telephone costs etc. and let us assume that it amounts to the following:

Fuel = $ 15 per month

Electricity = $10 per month

Administration = $2.50 x 4 hrs/month = $ 10 per month

Telephone = $2 per month

To get a more realistic figure for your particular circumstances, you may have to recalculate these figures.

Total other costs = $37.00 per month or $0.39 per hour

Divide the total monthly other costs by the total labor hours per month $37/96 = **$0.39** per hour.

Packaging is treated separately because the cost is known and depends on the type of product that will be used. In this case we will use a plastic bucket that holds 350 gr of cookies.

Packaging - $0.02 per bucket.

Calculating production cost for a specific recipe

To calculate the production cost for a specific recipe we will have to calculate the ingredient cost plus labor cost plus other costs related to that recipe to get the total cost to produce that recipe. Once we have the total production cost we can determine the selling price.

Step 1 – Determine the ingredient cost to produce cookies from a specific recipe.

To work out ingredient costs the ingredients indicated in a specific recipe must be broken down to the smallest measurement unit such as grams, milliliters, ounces, pints etc. Multiply the number of units by the unit price to get the cost of an ingredient. Add all the ingredient costs to get the total ingredient cost.

Let us take a recipe for baking chocolate cookies. The total bake time is 60 minutes and the total yield 1200 g of cookies. We will require 4 x 300 g plastic buckets for packaging.

The calculation of the total production cost for this recipe will be as follows:

Ingredient cost

Ingredients	Unit	Unit price	Total
Cake flour	500 gr	$0.005	$2.50
Baking powder	5 gr	$0.015	$0.07
Coconut	375 gr	$0.005	$1.87
Butter	250 gr	$0.006	$1.50
Castor sugar	250 gr	$0.002	$0.50
Cocoa	50 gr	$0.016	$0.80
Salt	5 gr	$0.001	$0.005
Brown Chocolate	100 gr	$0.015	$1.50
Total Ingredient cost			**$8.75**

Step 2 – Determine your labor cost for a specific recipe

Labor cost

Labor	Hours	Rate/hr	Total
Production hours	1	$5	$5.00
Operational hours	0.25	$5	$1.25
Total Labor cost			**$6.25**

Step 3– Determine other costs

We have established that the total other cost amount to $0.39 per hour.

A 1 liter plastic bucket with lid costs $0.20 each.

Other cost	Hours	Cost/unit	Total

Electricity, transport	1	$0.39	$0.39
Packaging	**Unit**	**Cost/unit**	**Total**
Bucket 300gr	4	$0.20	$0.80
Total other costs			**$1.19**

Step 4– Determine the total production cost

The total production cost is equal to the sum of all the cost elements of producing the cookies based on the prescribed recipe.

It is set out as follows:

Total Production Cost	Total
Ingredient cost	$8.75
Labor cost	$6.25
Other costs	$1.19
TOTAL PRODUCTION COST	**$16.19**

The cookie yield is 1200 grams and the cost per gram **$0.0135**

Calculating the selling price for a specific recipe

Now that we know the production cost of baking chocolate cookies, we can determine the selling price.

Step 5 – Calculate selling price

Divide the total production cost by the number of buckets you can make per hour ($16.19/4 = $4.05 per bucket). This is the minimum price that will cover your costs. There is no profit but it will give you compensation for your labor which is $6.25 per bake or $1.56 per bucket.

The question is whether you feel that this is adequate compensation for your efforts or should you add a profit. The question also arises whether the selling price of $4.05 is in line with the market price. Will people pay

$4.05 for a bucket? If the price is lower than the going rate, you can add a profit and compensate for a low labor rate. If the price is considerably higher than similar products, consider reducing your labor cost and/or increasing your production. If this is not possible then you should consider an alternative recipe that will reduce ingredient cost and labor cost.

Calculating profitability

Remember that a home business like any other business aims to make a profit. Calculating a selling price that will provide a reasonable profit for this particular recipe can be done as follows:

Cost Analysis	Unit	Cost/unit	Total
Total cost/bucket	300gr	$0.0135	$4.05
Mark-up 40%			$1.62
Selling price/tub	1		$5.67
No of tubs/bake	4	$5.67	$22.68
Net profit/bake	**($5.67-$4.05=$1.62 x 4)**		**$6.48**

If we assume that we can produce 2 bakes per hr or 16 bakes per day and we assume to work 3 days per week or 12 days per month, the net monthly income can be calculated as follows:

Net income per month = $6.48 x 16 = $103.68 x 12=$1 244.16 per month.

Since you are also the only worker the labor cost can be added to the profit to get the potential gross return per month = $6.48 + $6.25 = $12.73 x 16=$203.68 x 12 = $2444.16 per month.

The calculation shows the potential return but even if you only achieve 50% of the return it still gives you $1222.08 which is not too bad for working 12 days in a month.

b. Percentage Method

The second method of calculating your selling price is a short cut method that uses a percentage mark-up on the ingredient cost. In many industries a percentage of 40% to 50% is not unusual. In the food industry it is generally accepted that a 40% mark-up is realistic.

To set a price, simply multiply the ingredient cost by 2.5 (2.5 x 40% = 100%). Taking the example of the chocolate cookie, the ingredient cost is $8.75. Multiply $8.75 by 2.5 = $21.88 to produce 4 x 300 gr buckets. The selling price for 1 tub is **$5.47.** Compare this with the selling price of **$5.67** calculated with the production cost method and it is much the same.

The figure of 40% is a guideline and will be affected by the cost of ingredients and labor cost. The final decision should be based on being competitive and still making a decent return for your efforts.

Checking your competitors

This important information is required to determine a competitive price for your products. Make a point of regularly looking at candy and cookie prices in your local store and also check what flea market candy vendors charge for their products. Although you need not be cheaper than your competitors, it makes sense to be in the same price range. What is important is that you produce the highest quality product as is possible. Quality sells!

It is a good idea to check out prices on the internet. There are many web stores that sell cookies and candy and it is helpful to see what they charge. Another important factor to consider is the way in which your competitors present and promote their products. Do they provide for a particular niche? What type of packaging do they use? What can you do to be different from them?

4. PROFITABLE STARTER RECIPES

Many recipes are just too expensive to make a decent profit. The next number of cookie and candy recipes have been tested and proved to be successful with the customers that I deal with. You may not have the same degree of success but I do think that they are worth trying. Also keep in mind that you should limit the number of products that you produce so that quality and consistency can be maintained.

Cookie recipes

Ginger Cookie

Ginger bread is also one of those long time favorite cookies. The dense honey brown cookie has a distinct ginger taste but is not too strong. It is easy to make and will keep well for long time after being baked.

Ingredients:

250 g Margarine

250 ml (1 Cup) Corn syrup

2 Eggs

750 g (5 Cups) Cake flour

500 ml Brown sugar (2 cups)

30 ml Ground Ginger

10 ml Bicarbonate of Soda (2 t)

5 ml Salt (1 t)

75 ml Milk

Preparation:

- Melt the Margarine and stir in the syrup. Allow to cool.

- Beat in eggs one at a time. Sift together the dry ingredients and stir into the syrup mixture alternately with milk. Allow the dough to chill in the refrigerator until firm enough to shape.

- Roll out and cut into shape, or shape into small balls and press down with a fork. Place on a greased pan or baking sheet. Allow enough space for biscuits to expand.

- Bake in moderately hot oven (190 °C) for approximately 10 minutes.

Coconut Oatmeal Cookie

Oatmeal cookies are a proverbial favorite with both kids and adults. This recipe is loaded with oats, which produces a crisp and chewy cookie that you can also fill with chocolate chips (white or dark chocolate), dried fruits, and/or chopped nuts

Ingredients:

6 tbsp Cocoa powder

1 cup Flaked coconut

3 cups Oats (quick cooking)

1 stick Margarine

1/2 cup Milk

2 cups Sugar

1 tsp Vanilla extract

Preparation:

- Mix cocoa powder, coconut and oats in large bowl, set aside.

- In a saucepan, bring margarine, milk and sugar to boil, allowing to boil for 2 minutes, and then add vanilla extract.

- Pour the mixture over the oatmeal mixture, mixing well. Drop by teaspoonfuls onto waxed paper and allow setting until firm.

Sugar Spice Cookie

This is a crunchy and spicy traditional cookie. It is made a little differently than most cookie batters as it contains spices such as cloves, ginger, cinnamon and nuts in the recipe.

The dough does need to be chilled slightly. Upon removing it from the refrigerator you can roll it out and use cookie cutters to press out a variety of different cookie forms. The dough should be rolled out quite thin (±3 mm) as you want the baked cookies to have a snappy crunch but do not over bake or they will become too brittle. These store especially well and can be used as part of a cookie mix.

Ingredients:

1500g Flour

625 g Sugar

500 g Margarine

4 Eggs

1 tsp Crème of Tarter

1 tsp Bicarbonate of Soda

1 tsp Salt

1 tsp Cloves

1 tsp Ginger

1 tsp Cinnamon

1 tsp Ground nut

Preparation:

- Mix the dry ingredients and add sugar.

- Beat the eggs and add the dry mixture to form a stiff dough.
- Roll out the dough to about 3mm.
- Press out the cookies in different shapes and place on baking paper.
- Bake 10 – 15 minutes at 200°C.

Chocolate Cookie (Romany Creams)

This is a cocoa- and coconut-flavored cookie sandwiched with rich melted chocolate (depending on what kind of chocolate you use). These cookies have a dark color because of the cocoa and they melt in your mouth if they are made the right away because of their soft texture.

Ingredients:

500 ml Flour (2c)

5 ml Baking powder (1 tsp)

375 ml Coconut (1.5c)

250 g Margarine

250 ml Castor sugar (1c)

50 ml Cocoa (4)

Salt

60 ml boiling water

Brown Chocolate

Preparation:

- Mix the butter and sugar. Add flour, baking powder, salt and coconut.
- Dissolve the cocoa in hot water and add to mixture.

- Put teaspoonfuls on baking sheet

- Bake at 180°C for 15 minutes

- Melt the chocolate over boiling water in microwave oven and then spread between the cookies.

Candy recipes

The following candy recipes have been chosen because they are relatively easy to make and they have all proven to be popular homemade candies. There are also candy recipes that you do not have to boil sugar and only requires the mixing of ingredients. Our coconut ice recipe falls in this category. It is extremely simple to make and is a firm favorite with everybody.

Marshmallows

Marshmallows are a fluffy, light confection usually made from boiled sugar syrup whipped with gelatin and egg whites. If you've never made homemade marshmallows, you are in for a treat. Freshly made marshmallows are soft and subtly fragrant, while most store-bought marshmallows are more like chewy cardboard. Best of all, you can customize your marshmallows in a variety of shapes, sizes, colors, and flavors. This marshmallow recipe is unique because it is a *no bake* recipe. It only involves the mixing of the mixture with a hand beater until it reaches the desired state of firmness.

Ingredients:

60 ml Cold water (¼ c)

37 ml Gelatin (2 ½ tbsp)

185 ml boiling water (¾ c)

500 ml White sugar (2 c)

Pinch salt

1 Egg white

3 ml Vanilla essence (½ tsp)

Use toasted Coconut or Icing sugar and Corn flour for dusting.

Preparation:

- Pour 60 ml water into a large bowl, sprinkle over gelatin and leave to soak.

- Add the boiling water and stir until dissolved.

- Add sugar, egg white and salt. Beat with electric hand beater for 15 – 20 minutes until very stiff – to hold its shape. Add Vanilla essence for flavor.

- Divide the mixture into half. Color one half pink if desired.

- Sprinkle a layer of toasted coconut or sift layer of icing sugar and corn flour (2 parts to 1 part) into the base of a greased pan.

- Pour in the mixture. Dust with remaining toasted coconut or icing sugar mixture. Leave to set.

- Dip a knife into hot water. Dry, and then cut the mixture into 2.5 cm squares. Toss in coconut or dust with icing sugar mixture.

TIP

Store in airtight containers.

Coconut Ice

Coconut ice is always a favorite and it is really very simple to make because there is no baking involved. The basic ingredients are coconut and condensed milk. The ingredients are simply mixed together and pressed into a flat pan to produce a soft, sweet coconut candy.

Ingredients:

350 g Fine desiccated coconut

400 g icing sugar

1 tin Condensed milk

5 ml Vanilla essence

Food coloring.

Preparation:

- Place condensed milk in a bowl and add icing sugar and vanilla. Beat well then mix in the coconut. The mixture will get firm but persevere until everything is combined.

- Divide the mixture in two equal parts and add food coloring to one part. Put the white mixture into a flat tray 12 x 22 cm and press down evenly. Take the colored mixture and place on top of white mixture. Press down evenly.

- Leave to set over night.

- Cut into pieces 5cm x 8 cm and spread on a sheet of paper to dry slightly.

Turkish delight

Turkish delight comes in many different flavors: roses, lemon, ginger, Hazelnut. In fact, if you can think it, it can probably go into Turkish delight ... and then you can still coat it with chocolate if that takes your fancy. However, our recipe is made simple by covering the squares with a mixture of icing sugar and corn flour.

The actual production of Turkish delight is very easy. Basically, all you need to do is to make a sugar and water syrup and then add some gelatin and flavorings and leave everything to set. It really is that simple!

Ingredients:

40 g Gelatin

800g White sugar

70g Corn flour

Pinch salt

2.5 ml Citric acid

4ml Rose water

Red food coloring

Corn flour and Icing sugar for dusting

Preparation:

- Soak the gelatin in 100 ml water.
- Add 400 ml of water and stir in sugar, corn flour, salt and citric acid.
- Stir over low heat until the sugar has dissolved.
- Bring to boil and boil for 15 minutes over low heat.
- Turn off the heat and add food coloring and rose water.
- Pour into 12 x 22cm greased tray to thickness of 2 cm. Leave to cool over night, and then cut into 2 cm squares.
- Roll squares in equal parts of corn flour and icing sugar.

<u>TIPS</u>

Add gelatin to water and not other way around.

When cutting squares, put oil on knife and soak it in a glass of hot water to prevent it from sticking to the mixture.

Peanut Brittle

This is a crunchy candy with lots of peanuts. Not too sweet, not too hard, not sticky. This recipe will give you a truly delicious product that will have your customers raving for more.

Ingredients:

75 g Margarine

340 ml (1/2 cup) White sugar

125 ml (1/2 cup) Golden syrup

250 ml (1 cup) Boiling water

325 ml (1.5 cups) Salted peanuts.

Preparation:

- Put the margarine, sugar, syrup and water in a pot.
- Dissolve the sugar over low heat.
- Bring to boil and boil over medium heat for 30 min. – do not stir. (149°C - 154°C)
- To test, drop a little mixture in cold water. If ready, it will set hard and will crack when broken.
- Remove from heat and stir in nuts.
- Pour into a greased pan 12 x 22 cm and allow setting.
- Cut or break into pieces.

TIP

Wait for about 10 minutes (before cold), and cut into pieces 5 x 8 cm.

Fudge

Fudge is a favorite traditional candy that is loved by everyone. This can be a difficult product to make unless you use a candy thermometer to ensure that you boil the sugar mixture to the right consistency.

Ingredients:

4 cups White sugar

1 cup full cream milk

50 g Butter

2 tbsp Golden syrup

1 tin Condensed milk

1 tsp Vanilla essence

Preparation:

- Prepare a saucepan 20 x 16 cm by greasing.

- Pour the milk into a heavy saucepan.

- Add butter, castor sugar and golden syrup and stir over low heat until sugar has dissolved. Brush down the sides of the pan with hot water from time to time

- Boil for 5 minutes while stirring constantly

- Add condensed milk and bring to boil. Cook for 15 minutes stirring continuously until the mixture reaches temperature of 112 °C on thermometer.

- Remove from the heat and wait until bubbles subside. Stir in vanilla and beat with a wooden spoon until the mixture is thick and creamy and a heavy tail is formed when the mixture is allowed to fall from the spoon.

- Pour the mixture into the pan and allow cooling. When set, mark the fudge with an oiled knife. Cut when completely cool and keep in airtight container.

Recipe profitability comparison

These cookie and candy recipes have been tested for consistency and in the following discussion we will compare the profitability of each recipe. This type of exercise makes it possible to critically judge each recipe and if they do not meet your requirements, can be replaced by a more profitable recipe.

Table 1 – Recipe cost analysis

PRODUCT	Units/ Pack	No of Packs	Cost/ Pack	Sell/ Pack	Profit/ Pack	% Profit
CANDY						
Turkish Delight	1	12	$0.40	$0.70	$0.30	70%
Peanut Brittle	1	10	$0.25	$0.50	$0.25	100%
Marshmallows	20	3	$0.94	$1.00	$0.06	6%
Coconut Ice	6	9	$0.48	$1.00	$0.52	108%
Fudge (Vanilla)	6	9	$0.46	$1	$0.54	117%
Fudge (white chocolate)	6	9	$0.57	$1	$0.43	75%
Fudge(brown chocolate)	6	9	$0.57	$1	$0.43	75%
COOKIES						
Spice cookie	350 g	5	$1.09	$2.00	$0.91	83%
Shortbread	300 g	4	$0.92	$1.50	$0.58	63%
Ginger cookie	350 g	4	$1.10	$1.50	$0.40	36%
Coconut cookie	316 g	3	$1.39	$2.00	$0.61	44%
Romany Creams	300 g	3	$2.05	$2.50	$0.45	22%

From the analysis in table 1 it seems that in general, candy is more profitable than cookies. Not all products are equally profitable. Under candies the top performers are peanut brittle, coconut ice and fudge. Marshmallows are the least profitable. Top performers under cookies are traditional spice cookies and shortbread. The least profitable are Romany Creams.

The most obvious factors influencing profitability include items such as the yield, the cost of ingredients and labor cost. For instance Romany Creams are "sandwich" cookies requiring extra labor to put two cookies together. Marshmallows do not have a big enough yield to make it profitable.

Another consideration is the fact that certain products are widely available in stores and other outlets. It is impossible to compete with the price of mass produced products. The way around this is to add something to make the product unique. Adding ingredients such as chocolate, nuts etc can make a big difference.

It should be remembered that this is a theoretical exercise and that a product with a top rating will not necessarily be a good seller. In my experience a unique homemade and versatile product like fudge has the best chance of being a good seller. It also makes sense to have a few products to start out with and to see what results can be obtained before making a final decision about product choice.

5. HOW TO PROMOTE YOUR PRODUCTS

There are a number of important things that you can do to promote your products. Some are discussed here.

Branding and labeling

Although you are only developing a home business, it is essential that your products create a professional image. For this reason it is important to develop your own "brand" of product so that your customers will associate it with quality and good price. Think of a catchy name for your products and spend some money on a label that you can put on your product. This will definitely put you ahead of your competitors and keep in mind that you do not have to spend a lot of money to achieve a professional look.

To comply with health regulations you will have to provide the following minimum information:

Product name

Name and address of manufacturer

A list of ingredients

Price

Packaging

Packaging is a very important promotion angle. Please do not skimp on this item. Ordinary plastic bags are cheap but do not do justice to the hard work that you have put in to produce a quality product. The container plays a major part in selling your product! I have experimented with different types of packaging and have standardized on a transparent plastic tub of 1 liter for cookies and plastic boxes and small polypropylene bags for candy bars. When you use a poly prop bag it must be sealed properly with a bag sealer.

Another advantage of using high quality packaging is that your customer will buy it as a gift because it looks great. You can also charge more because the product looks more professional. Customers today are also very health conscious and demand safe and healthy products. Securely wrapped and sealed packages are vital.

Advertising

Advertising can become very expensive and I would suggest that you decide on an acceptable budget before you start. Consider putting a small ad in your local newspaper and watch your sales grow. Another idea is to send out a flyer to your local community.

This should not cost you much and if you can target a specific niche such as promoting your products for children's parties, birthdays etc. you will be sure to get good results. Advertising should be part of an overall marketing plan.

Gift Baskets and Bouquets

Cookie gift baskets and bouquets are becoming very popular and is an ideal way of adding value to your products and opening up new ways of selling your products. They make excellent gifts and can be linked to special occasions such as birthdays, births etc.

Some tips to make Gift Baskets

Gift baskets are extremely easy to assemble, but the final result looks stunning - a true labor of love (without the 'labor'). Suitable for any occasion, unique gift baskets can often be just the solution when you can't decide on a particular gift item. You can use different shapes of baskets, with or without a handle, and the size depends on what you want to put into it.

Here's How:

- Decide what the basket 'theme' will be first, then look for a sufficiently sized basket.
- Cut 2 yards of cellophane and lay it on the table surface, right side down, and place the basket in the middle of it.
- Arrange all items inside the basket; you can place a cloth napkin or paper doily in the bottom. Ensure that breakable items are secured or wrapped in cloth or tissue to prevent breakage. Position tall items in the centre, with medium items on the outside, and small

ones in between. Individually-wrapped candy sprinkled throughout the items, adds a nice sweet touch.

- Gather up the cellophane, pulling up the short sides first, then longer sides, and secure with a long twist tie. A helper is great for this step.
- Add the ribbon, making a nice bow with long curved tails. Or attach a ready-made bow. No need to remove the twist tie.
- Attach the gift tag with string or tape it to the front cellophane.
- If one of the short sides of cellophane is gaping, you may be able to adjust it by pulling gently on the top section, or secure with a small piece of clear tape.
- Resist the urge to 'play' with the cellophane to get it just right - the idea is to gather the cellophane which produces an array of varying sizes of cellophane 'petals' - a unique 'bouquet'. If the 'petals' are too long for your liking, you can trim them with scissors.

Tips:

Cellophane is sold in clear, colored, print or festive. The clear with a small gold pattern is very versatile for any occasion.

Ready-made bows are great for taking the hassle out of making one, but make sure that the size is right for the basket - a large basket requires a larger bow. Likewise, don't hide a small basket with an oversized bow.

Other items can be used instead of a basket, such as a casserole dish, pie plate, serving bowl, or gift box bottom. If the basket or container has very low sides, you may require a helper to gather up the cellophane. The gift tag can be attached by a string from the gathered bow, or taped to the front of the basket.

Cookie Bouquet

A cookie gift bouquet makes a great surprise treat for anyone who likes cookies. It can be as simple or intricate as you'd like, depending on your abilities and time. You can even create personalized cookies to make your gift more memorable. A cookie gift bouquet makes a great gift for a special occasion (Father's Day, Birthday, Grandparents gift, etc.).

The first thing you'll need for your bouquet is a mug. It is best to use a standard ceramic mug with a solid base. You can either purchase a new mug for your occasion or use your gift recipient's favorite coffee mug for a special treat. Buy a small piece of floral foam, available at most craft stores, and cut the foam in the shape of cylinder to fit in the mug. It should be snug, but you shouldn't have to force the foam into the mug. Cut the foam to be about an inch shorter than the height of the mug. Place some color-coordinated shred in the mug and stuff it around the cracks of the foam so that it remains in place.

The next step is to bake some cookies for your bouquet. Depending on the size of the cookies, 3 to 6 will likely be plenty. Wrap each cookie in colored plastic wrap to match your gift theme. Attach wooden bamboo skewers to the back of each cookie using clear tape.

To finish your bouquet, all you need to do is carefully push the wooden skewers into the floral foam. You may need to trim the skewers to make them the right height. Make each cookie a different height for the best presentation. Attach a small bow to the mug and you're all done.

6. HOW TO FIND A MARKET

To find a market for your products might seem difficult in the beginning, but once you start thinking about the many options, it will be necessary to draw up a marketing strategy along the lines indicated below.

Apart from the obvious selling to friends and family, you should also think of the following options to market and sell your products:

Local shops

The first that you can try to do with your bake goods, is bake some samples that you can take to various smaller local coffee shops. I know that in most areas you can easily find a small locally owned coffee shop that either bakes their own goods or has to order them from a supplier. In my experience, most locally owned coffee shops would prefer to purchase the baked goods from a local person rather than have to pay for the shipping and cost of their supplier or have to worry about the supplier deciding to stop carrying a product.

Flea Markets and Farmer's Markets

The second place that you might want to investigate selling your baked goods at would be going to local flea markets or farmers markets. However, first find out what specific regulations are applicable and what you will have to pay for a stall. Some flea markets will charge you a percentage (e.g. 10%) of your total sales for the day, and others may charge you straight fee for the day. So you will want to ask about this when you call to inquire about a space at a flea market. To make money with your own flea market business you need to have good quality flea market products (such as these that we are recommending) at reasonable prices. But the other ingredient that is often overlooked is that you have to have the ability to outsell your competition. I have been selling my cookies and candy on flea markets for a long time and my experience is that you must provide quality products at reasonable prices and have a good spot that will get good flow of traffic past your stall.

Here are tips that you can use to outsell your flea market competitors:

Tips for selling on flea markets

Tip 1

Customer service is crucial. People want to be treated well, regardless of where they are shopping. Be the flea market vendor that is known for friendliness and helpfulness. Shoppers will be glad to buy from you, even if your prices are the same as other flea market vendors.

Tip 2

Always have an organized and pleasant flea market booth. Shoppers will enjoy visiting your booth if your merchandise is displayed nicely. Good signage at strategic points and product prices that are clearly displayed will provide that professional look that people are drawn to.

Tip 3

Keep track of other vendor's prices. Your prices should always be at, or below their prices. Even if lowering your prices cuts into your profits you need to adjust them. You can always make up the lost profit on higher sales.

Tip 4

Be positive. Shoppers want to buy from positive sellers. Shopping at a flea market is supposed to be fun, make it fun for your customers.

Tip 5

Introduce a new variety of items. If shoppers know that you always have a nice variety of new products at your flea market booth, they will go to you first to see what new products you have. Make sure that the products you introduce fit into your current merchandise. You want your customers to know you for a certain product category. A product that goes well with candy and cookies is dried fruit. If you can find a good quality product at a reasonable price you can consider adding that to your range.

Selling on the Internet

The third place that you could try selling your bake goods is on the internet. You will find that apart from specific e- stores, there are some offerings on e-Bay and Bid or Buy in South Africa.

Setting up your own Website

If you are new to the internet, this might be difficult to achieve but there are many options to consider.

Firstly, you could start a blog and write about your products.

Secondly, you could inform friends and family of you home business by setting up an e-mail campaign.

Thirdly, you could take up the offer of many free website providers on the net to set up your own website. You will find many options on the internet.

They not only will they provide you with a free website but they also provide free hosting. This means that you can start your own website without spending one cent.

7. HOME BAKING RESOURCES

To assist you with the development of your home bake business, the following helpful information will help you to avoid costly mistakes.

Storing and Freezing Your Cookies

Here are some tips for freezing and storing your cookies:

- *Cooling down* - make sure your cookies are completely cool before preparing them for storage or freezing. Any frosting or icing should also be fully set and firm.
- *Storing* - cookies should be stored in airtight containers. Some cookies will keep better if individually wrapped, such as very large gourmet type cookies, large cutout and frosted cookies and very thick cookies. Plastic wrap, foil or waxed paper works well for individually wrapping the cookies.
- *Freezing* - in general most cookies will freeze well and can last for up to 1 year from when you baked them. Make sure the cookies are wrapped well in waxed paper, plastic wrap or foil. Wrap them individually to make them last longer, hold their shape better and preserve their taste and texture. Then put them in an airtight container like a Tupperware or other container. You can also use a Ziploc freezer bag; just make sure you have sealed it tightly. Cookies that have been frosted will only keep for a few months in the freezer.
- *Defrosting cookies* - unwrap the cookies carefully and let them thaw completely and come to room temperature before serving. You can also microwave them on high for about 20-30 seconds.
- *Freezing cookie dough* - cookie dough can be frozen for up to 1 month. Make the cookie dough in a ball and wrap it with waxed paper. When you want to use it again, let it thaw out completely before preparing to bake. This can save a lot of time and give you the same fresh from the oven taste as fresh baked cookies. Very soft dough should not be frozen. Place the dough in an airtight container or freezer bag. Cookie dough can be kept for up to 3 months before use.

- When freezing any food article, it is a good idea to write the freezing date on the article.

Write a Business plan

One of the best things you can do for yourself before you start your business is to sit down and write your business plan. Many people who want to start a home business ask if they really NEED a business plan, to which I ask if they really NEED to start a home business. Writing a business plan for your home based business should be considered essential for many reasons, the most obvious of which is that a business plan is required if you are going to seek funding.

A business plan will also help you gain focus and think through each aspect of your business. It will also help you remain focused when you get discouraged or feel overwhelmed. You can figure out how to deal with possible problems before they occur.

Business plans will vary widely, depending upon what type of business you have, so what may work well for one business may not be suitable for another.

Your business plan doesn't have to be very long, but does have to present you and your business, goals - both short and long term, intentions, and detailed information about your business, in the very best possible light.

Elements of a Business Plan Include:

- *Your objectives.* What exactly do you want to accomplish? What are your goals for your business?
- *Describe your business.* What is your legal structure? When was it formed? Who owns and operates it?
- *Define your market.* What are you going to sell? A product or service? Or both? You'll want to describe exactly what is going to be sold. Is there a need for your product or service? Who are you selling to? Why will your business have a competitive edge over other businesses? Do you have a niche?

- **Explain how you intend to meet those needs.** How will you produce the product/service? How will your customers receive your goods?
- **Define your staff,** or suppliers, if any.
- **Make a time table.** Do you expect to reach a certain goal in a specific amount of time?
- **Calculate and clearly state your financial requirements.** How much capital will it cost you to get the materials you need to start-up? Give detailed information about how the capital will be spent.
- **Licenses or fees?**
- **Advertising?**
- **Operations.** Operate your business until you see a profit?
- **Delivery.** How will you deliver your product or service?
- **Subcontractors?**
- **Pay staff?**
- **Sales forecast**
- **Profit and loss**
- **Sales and marketing strategy**

If you make a mistake in this area, by all means count on needing more than you actually will. Many terrific home businesses have ground to a screeching halt because they ran out of operating money too soon.

Conversion tables

The following tables are useful to have handy when you are baking or making candy.

Dry ingredients weight

1 oz = 1/16 lb = 30 g

4 oz = ¼ lb = 120 gr

8 oz = ½ lb = 240 g

12 oz = ¾ lb = 360 g

16 oz = 1 lb = 480 g

Note: To convert ounces to grams, multiply the number of ounces by 30.

Cup conversions

1 Cup flour = 140 g

1 Cup rice = 150 g

1 Cup sugar = 190 g

1 Cup castor sugar = 200 g

1 Cup icing sugar = 140 g

1 Cup dark brown sugar = 150 g

1 Cup light brown sugar = 216 g

1 Cup butter = 200 g

1 Cup nuts = 105 g

1 Cup dried fruit = 190 g

1 Cup raisins = 190 g

1 Cup dry coconut = 78 g

1 Cup cocoa = 80 g

1 Cup bran = 40 g

Liquid conversions

¼ tsp = 1 ml

½ tsp = 2 ml

1 tsp = 5 ml

3 tsp = 1 tbl = ½ fluid oz = 15 ml

2 tbl = ⅛ cup = 1 fl oz = 30 ml

4 tbl = ¼ cup = 2 fl oz = 60 ml

8 tbl = ½ cup = 4 fl oz = 120 ml

12 tbl = ¾ cup = 6 fl oz = 180 ml

16 tbl = 1 cup = 8 fl oz = 240 ml

1 pt = 2 cups = 16 fl oz = 480 ml

1 qt = 4 cups = 32 fl oz = 960 ml

33 fl oz = 1000 ml = 1 liter

Oven temperatures

	Fahrenheit,	Celsius,	Gas mark,
Freeze water,	32°F	0°C	
Room temperature,	68°F,	20°C,	
Boil water,	212°F,	100°C,	
	325°F	160°C	3,
	350°F	180°C	4
Bake,	375°F	190°C	5
	400°F	200°C	6
	425°F	220°C	7
	450°F	230°C	8

Length

1 in = 2.5 cm

6 in = 15 cm

12 in = 1 ft = 30 cm

36 in = 3 ft = 1 yd = 90 cm

40 in = 100 cm = 1 m

8. CONCLUSIONS

A home bake business can be started with relative ease and if you have an interest in baking, the recipes in this book will prove to be real money spinners. No specialized equipment is needed since most of the items you will already have in your kitchen. The only thing that you need to do is to start rolling!

Finding a market for home bake products is also not that difficult provided that you produce quality products and that you keep to your promises. The best part of this type of home business is that you can start small and keep costs low. As you gain in experience you can gradually expand and become more professional.

You may not become a millionaire but you will make money and have the satisfaction of producing a product that everybody loves.

www.ingramcontent.com/pod-product-compliance
Lightning Source LLC
Chambersburg PA
CBHW031928240526
45464CB00023B/2685